First Words

First Words
Poems

Emily Vogel

NQ Books™

The New York Quarterly Foundation, Inc.
New York, New York

NYQ Books™ is an imprint of The New York Quarterly Foundation, Inc.

The New York Quarterly Foundation, Inc.
P. O. Box 2015
Old Chelsea Station
New York, NY 10113

www.nyq.org

First Edition

Set in New Baskerville

Layout by Mickey Kellam

Cover Design by Raymond P. Hammond

Cover Illustration: "Turned Cartwheels 'cross the Floor"
4" x 5.5" oil on watercolor paper, by Marco Muñoz Jaramillo
http://mmjaramillo.wix.com/marcomunozjaramillo

Library of Congress Control Number: 2015908382

ISBN: 978-1-63045-016-8

First Words

Acknowledgments

"A Small Report" first appeared in *Contemporary Literary Horizons*.

"Is" first appeared in *Tiferet*.

"Sequestering" and "An Ear, The Forest, Or?" first appeared in *Omniverse*.

"A Child's Mouth" first appeared in *2 Bridges Review*.

"Dear Clare" first appeared in *Paterson Literary Review*.

Contents

For Clare, and Joseph, the eternal fisherman, and for the angel Gabriel, who was then only thought, seed—all once starlight—and still now sustaining—ad infinitum.

Dawn, Again

1
Before dawn: a dark window, opaque
as the space which houses the brain.
A gnat circles my coffee cup, lands on the rim
over and over again, obstinate
and wont to tendency. Death is a substance
for generating meaningful acts of language.

2
The silence is elaborate with vacancies.
Yesterday I bought canned goods at the grocery store
and then last night
I dreamt I was buying canned goods
at the grocery store. You crept into bed beside me
last night, clean as a shadow, full of human breath.

3
The self is the pull of the moon. It desires itself,
like a reflection, and also wants to remain oblivious.
I forget things that I later remember as things
that were once supposed to be important.
I have tasks. Tasks, I tell you!
Every time you write, you embody water,
inevitable as a river. I cannot stop you
from moving into the future.

4
Somewhere they were discussing boiled eggs
and fish. It sounded romantic, like something
that suffers, and I mentioned it. You like to see things
that are familiar as repetitions. These things
are as permanent as numbers.

5
There are no more metaphors
which pertain to grief. I want to offer you
an empty street, scarcely lit,
which only remembers the rain.
Eventually, you will hear music,
an hour will turn like the dawn,
and you will have to go on.

A Small Report

Jesus was crucified yesterday afternoon, or Jesus was crucified
two thousand years ago. The days pass

in the usual sense of days passing:

we eat pork roast and potatoes,
watch clever commercials on the television.

The nature of time is terrifically troubling.

A six-foot Santa rises among some evergreen trees,
among the muck of a dimly lit back road,
among the cold and forthcoming season.

You fall asleep on the floor beneath my feet.
Somewhere is the sound of water.
My womb swells with the bulk of a life.
Stories unfold in a series of images,
people pass in and out as personalities
bereft of names.

At the falling of dusk, Emmanuel comes,
and the traffic on the highway proceeds

in a wild confusion of light.

First Snow

The beginning of winter this year
is a strange euthanasia of gray, as we drive
along the highway, the dusk forthcoming
as the language of our casual tongues.
I realize that you are the essence of song
in a warm room.

This is how we return to one another,
like seasons, comfortable as voices,
as accumulations of various years.
The snow is timely, and yet sudden,
a reason to dwell like an eye
that squints into a glimmer of light.

The Incident

Like a lot of things, the sea is inexhaustible.
As well, the days are full of a perpetual sleep,
some trembling threshold
of a lost and aimless language, all of it gone
astray like a drifting planet, automatic
as some usual reflex of the body.

Yes, it is almost agreeable to go on talking like this.
The road looks dense with dusk.
The world is an endless proposition, a shit-pile,
a blessed heaven that awaits. It contends
with useless garbage, opportunities for mercy,
misunderstandings, things tirelessly
both beautiful and stupid.

God bless all its luxuries of shorthanded involvements.
They're itemized, effective, love simulated
in digital increments. They have no idea
what screaming is, what the moon
from a third story window can evoke.

On the TV, perfect people are fucking.
My husband is mentioning various and relevant scenarios,
fantastic and fragmented things
which remind me of the past, of purposeful
and needful aspects: abundant sun,
and the bleakest snow.

We are all an inevitable fall, an eternal compensation.
I don't remember. I don't remember.
I like the way he appears as he sleeps.
This: the unseeing eye of the incident,
untimed and unaccountable.

Breaking

The sensation of pain is incomprehensible to an infant, until
it is no longer incomprehensible.
Eventually it fails to elude her,
becomes as regular as variations of light and dark.
The world infiltrates as repetitions, enumerations, conversations
sustained by gradually familiar voices.
In a dark kitchen at 3 am, her mother breaks
in the sense that pain might break
amid the silent rooms of absolute solitude.
Also, a song plays somewhere about something breaking,
like a heart, or the first dawn.

Listening to Schumann in the Afternoon

Romance: a blood that sings in A minor on an unlikely afternoon.
I've meaning to tell you that automobiles are conducive
to most episodic weeping. God: the blinding sun
that follows the Eve of a recent birth.

Something has surfaced. In other words,
the December air explains everything.

There are obviously drastic notions
which allow you to believe
that you are most alive.

Each time I look at you, something wrenches,
everything contorted and true.

The days are sleepless, oblivious.
They pass like spirits in stagnant rooms.

How I revel in the imminent dark, wait anxiously
over and over, for the living eye
of tacit recognition.

Poem for my Week-Old Daughter

In a lapse of lucidity, you focus on a shape
made by a certain light, your eyes held captive
by the waking world. Your tiny jaw drops, your mouth
filling with new and unfamiliar air.
You are attuned to peripheries, a certain threshold
of looming sadness, which by now
is merely inarticulate—a perplexing
and irretrievable aspect.

Channel 3

The deepest part of the night is blue noise,
the sound of an infant breathing.
My husband snores beside her on the floor.
Me, I'm an unfathomable crater on the moon,
a vessel that contains conceivable things.
I want to lie in a field of waving wheat
and discuss the mysteries of the universe.
I travel through starlight which appears
on channel 3, my mind a conduit
for traversals, each evasion of the bleeding heart
a fleeting redemption.

Calamity

Because I didn't go looking for the moon last night,
I can't be sure. I made pork chops. They were offensive.
They rendered me a less apt woman. The guests were merciful,
entertaining, scholarly. I hid in the living room, weeping.
My daughter's mouth was open, shaped like a world,
and searched and searched
to be filled.

While the Religious Channel Was On

It seems they are merely conceptual.
Not people with lives and with whom I have exchanged words.
On the TV, they toil and toil under the beating sun.
Under surveillance.
Under the sign of the eternalized cross.

*

Computers are susceptible to discrepancies.
When I think of the Holy Spirit, administrative tasks
seem irrelevant. Corruption is ever-present,
but is perhaps flagrantly unintentional.
My little daughter stuffs her little mouth
with her fist.

*

Sometimes you soften, your soul placid,
as if mute as moonlight. Somewhere,
the ocean is a deaf hush, and children are safe and warm
in the ephemeral rushing of dreams.

*

Sanctus. Sanctus Dominus. Sanctus Dominus Deus.
Sometimes a flame can be so slight.

*

Love is the distance in a room.
My narrative proceeds like an eventual day,
like the nebulous eye of infancy.

*

Bread of life, consume me
the way a word can sometimes consume me.
Let me be hungry, embody the hunger itself:
the way a man or woman is occasionally helpless,
the way an infant might cry out
in the dead of night.

White Christmas

Incidentally, they're all singing Irving Berlin.
It's delightfully ironic. Their voices are small.
Their faces reflect certain dimensions of apprehension.
Christmas is soon upon us, and there is no snow.
There is the perpetual dream of snow.
I remember once, a long time ago, something crashing,
the dark avenues of the mind, and plentitudes of snow.

*

The saxophones are grand spectacles, instruments
which evoke a certain glad nostalgia. The children
have no idea what this means.
They cannot frame a reference, they know no snow
which expands across distances, no antiquation
of anything romantic. They imagine guns,
bank accounts, the magic of a blinking digit.

*

The conductor has wild arms. To cue the tuba,
he makes a motion like the trunk of an elephant.
It is good to "make noise" but the noise
must be mapped by the appropriate parameters.
Teachers holler until their voices are hoarse
from exhaustion.

*

Children are curious and condemned.
Christmas is soon upon us, and there is no snow.
I drive home in the imminent dusk, return to you,
and throw my whole self into the sanctum of your arms.
Inside our house, an unwitting infant sleeps,
and for now, knows only the sound of traffic, passing
in the unlikely December rain.

Is

An infant is a feeling like a cornfield in October,
in a dome of silence, hued with fiery light.

I've seen visions such as this
through car windows, swiftly passing.

A husband is built for the coldest winter.
He is a deep song heard through a ceiling.
He is a dream that has difficulty recalling itself.

A poet is stupid like an ape.
A poet is a painting that hangs cockeyed on a wall.

A mother is round, like any object.
Her body is made to twist like pain,
her spirit to laugh and rejoice
like April rivers.

A Ghostly Notion

I know that the flow of time is purposeful
by evidence of baseball fields seen from four flights up,
from out of the air. I am a child
and I'm standing in the rain in my socks.

My grandmother was a woman of few words.
My grandfather fought wars, sold lingerie,
was good for a good gag. My little daughter
lives in the stark light of futurity.

The world is an endless invention.
It is afflicted with scientific notions, love like soda-pop
and colorful balloons, symmetry and spandex.

The Sea of Galilee is in me. Contradiction is in me.
The desires of the God-fearing are in me.

The expanding sky fills me with visions,
my mind simultaneously located, pervasive and uncontained,
possible like a dream, and not round,
nuanced and gray, like a brain.

Beginnings

I have been witness to the beginning of the world—
how it reeled and railed out of the darkest ambiguities,
wailing like an infant, desperate as a seed.

It arose as life made by way of sacrifice,
straight from the barrel of a impetuous gun.

It cried Christ—as if to be saved once again
by the gentle to and fro
of a rocking cradle,

amid the hard air of winter,
summer—not referential, not even a mere dream.

It withstood noise, the junk of language and voices.

Also, there were slight questions
upon visions of light, upon ceilings, and people
that passed like blurry shapes
through rooms.

Christmas Poem 2012

I cradle the small body of our first born child,
and thus cradle the whole of your ancestry.
It is the thought of love, made manifest
and intimate as an eye.

Meanwhile, someone or something
is plucking harp strings: an occasional angel,
the dead once loved, or the heart itself.

Among this place is a strain of tears,
something ancient and almost ugly, like a city,
or a history: a vast and abominable population.

It is full of blood and song. It is full of aspiring souls,
those who traverse along yellow roads, out of necessity,
out of thirst for immense rivers.

I imagine it transcending, like a memory
of nowhere I have ever been. It ascends
like a vacillating star, a resurrection,
something imperfect, and thus sacred.

It is Christmas Eve, and the world is constant as a flame,
and we do not dare to go anywhere
other than here, and all thought of death or life
is as distanced and impossible
as some faint and elusive skyline.

Snowstorm 2012

If my daughter's first memory is of snow
and the ambient sound of Westerns on the TV,
let some God make that a holy mapping.

She has been born into an age of biblical proportions,
of improvised violence, of abundant theories,
and honest attempts at ameliorations,
however futile and absurd.

I have no inclination to blame and accuse.
I am compelled to committed acts of clemency,
to the wandering and evanescent Jesus.

How I long for the most verdant world.

How it turns and turns in an endless spell of lethargy,
indefinite and filled with smoke and desire:
any careening nation, oceans expanding like death,
and then all its trembling thresholds
of restoration or destruction.

Little one, I cannot take you outside
in the terrible quiet of this storm, this blight
sheathed in an ethereal winter.

Sequestering

There are sound barriers among abundances of snow. From the house, I can hear a man's voice like a distant shotgun. My newborn daughter gasps delightedly at the sight of an inanimate object. She smiles as she sleeps. The world is otherwise full of concrete and rumors all about zombies. Others claim that God is definitely a hoax of the highest order. A clock determines all relevant narratives. You are drowsy. You laugh as you watch very old movies. This sequestering from the snow is a type of indemnity, a reason not to get shot to death on an ordinary day at the supermarket. Meanwhile, the world is desperate to go on existing, and God's unassailable love is on many desperate radios.

An Infant's Conception

If there is no God, then the morning does not arrive.
Swarms of morning fog do not lift. I have seen dust swirl
in the yellow light
that falls in through cathedral windows.

*

Even while the book of windy pages turns,
nobody knows anything further about the issue.

It sifts like words, evanescing, things proclaimed
and then questioned.

It is like an infant's conception:
the disorderly world.

*

Some say
our salvation is mapped in the stars.
Mythologies consume us; history deceives us.
We make the most sense that we can
out of our helpless narratives.

We purchase automobiles and shoes
and condominiums
for the sake of our mortal desire.

It is sharp like an eye, bleeds like a pore.

*

Existence compels us to the business of business:
a desperate undertaking. It makes sense,
like an object,
named and signified.

Of course, mathematics is one way of explaining it,
but also audible breath, the sensation of water.

Nothing beyond these things.

*

The heartbeat that thrums in a mother's breast,
the comfort of soil, dissipation of air,
eventual glimpses of light.

*

You sleep beside me
like an idea with a brain. I think
I can hear the groan of your soul.

Your body is warm,
and most things otherwise
are irrelevant.

Just listen to the slight noise
of our newborn child: how language
is trying to make itself.

Just Night

Inside the mind of an infant, language blooms.
Whole cities are built. Soon, she is arrested
by visions, worlds
in the mundane corners of rooms.

My husband holds her on his chest, takes her weight
like a continent. The house
is dim with inactivity,
and yet the television prevails like a war.

Politicians prattle. Outside, there are inklings
of buoyant snow, something in the air, distanced as time.

And then night once again—that deep and awful lake,
life hovering over its slow surface,

or maybe
nothing of this at all,
aside from its vague conception.

Like some Babylonian mythology,
the world endures itself
like some perpetual pop song.

The world began and ended in autumn,
when a leaf vacillated in air
and touched the earth,

tentative as breath in a dark room,
when everyone and everything
is sleeping.

A Kind of Compassion

On certain evenings, I purge whole cities
of their rampant chaos. Their pollutions spread
as do misfired words. The cities are houses,
and the houses are on fire, and you continue
to sing fantastic songs, transgressive songs
whose high notes hit the air just like the fire
which consumes the houses, makes them
bleed like dutiful labors of the soul,
afflictions which cause angry jugulars
to throb. As the houses burn and burn,
a child wails out of confusion,
and the city gets lost
in its own confusion of constructs.
You are trying to quell all noise, your mind
a fire which suspects its own intelligence,
a madwoman screaming inside an attic
and a blind man that rescues her
as they fall like so many nights
into the underbrush. Such is the gravity of bodies.
Before you go to sleep, you carefully
hang your belt on the doorknob, place your hat,
like a habit, on the floor.

Wings

The world is a desert's trajectory.
Time, like the sunlight,
is vast and extravagant, and in the air
the souls of the dead swarm
invisible and vague as origins,
strangled by their own aspiring voices.

Meanwhile, our ears are attuned
to telepathic yearnings.
We long to sing drunkenly
on porches
subsumed by midnight,
under the deaf
and temporary moon.

And how we endure, like mothers:
pain, a happy deflection,
a day filled with schedules
and tidy compensations.

Dusk falls outside the window
and in a scene on the television,
and I ask
if you know the difference.
Communication is rapturous
and then falters, disintegrates.
I want to make love to you
wearing a Russian hat, and a coat
with fur on the collar.

Then suddenly
it is dark now too soon,
far too densely.
You are standing at the window,
waiting, holding a child

in your arms.
The child wails
upon arrivals.
God binds
like a molecule.
Pretense proliferates
in public places.
I am a paragon
of illustrious gloom.
The child wails
upon departures.

I recall once leaving the earth,
traveling upward and upward,
not in terror
nor in disbelief.

On Certain Educations

The sequential world is one way to accommodate.
I think about infrastructures
and the friendliness
of the common everyday living room.
I think about the smell of sex, the flaws and failures
of certain educations. As I try to console
the cry of an inconsolable infant. As I sip champagne
on a Thursday evening, gather immensities of garbage
to leave at the roadside on garbage night.
As the consolation becomes an investment,
like the intimacy of each void
which roots in the core of any human,
climbs upward through the soul,
through the throat, echoes
amid the mouth's sonorous caverns.
It is unrelenting, like the whir
of a modern kitchen appliance. On the radio,
a voice is a box like a talking brain.
I recall the first light of morning,
time defied by its own requirements,
God filling the winter air, and then vanishing
into the day's regular drudgery: a school bus
huffing its exhaustion
along the distances of those
once promising and enduring roads.

Briefly, Springtime

The opposite of winter
is still a dark spell,
an accident with coffee
on a Sunday morning.
My mother sends messages
along the scarce and unseeing lines
of cyberspace.
It felt for the first time
like spring today
and I was fiercely disappointed.
The grass and the air
were new and ebullient.
My daughter has fortitude
like a train.

*

On the television
are skeleton-women
and artful representations of malice.
They are loud, demoralizing, entertaining,
a reason to laugh and sip wine
in living rooms. The world
is a constant exchange,
the Bard's best estimate.
There is no economy in heaven.

*

The cinema will kill you.
Viruses will kill you.
Distance will kill you.
It will nourish your soul.

*

Memories of women, apparitions of women
drift like grievances
through your dreams, your literature.
They are wounds
which nourish your soul.
On our first date, you ate soup
and we rode across Central Park
in a carriage. We wandered
like blind men, oblivious lovers.

*

Later, an extremely tall woman sang out
serious as the darkness. There was a scarcity
of milk. Food spoiled.
There was a great improvement
in methods of transportation.
Then there were ordinary resurrections,
which rose like sunlight.
We did not pack our things, nor move
from location to location.
We endured like wrath
and the accumulation of bottles.
We were indebted to the earth.
We were obliged to occasions
of language. My daughter,
at one month old
was all efforts of understanding.
We passed through illusions of time
like determinations.
Briefly, my love, do not
grieve nor disdain me.

Why My Personal Narrative is Impertinent

Where gratitude is scarce, winter
is as brutal as a heartless fuck.
Not me, postpartum: gazing in church
one Tuesday morning
at the sunlight
cast through the stained glass.

Not me, not me: glad as a new lamb.

Generally, things are looking up.
The weather has been basically pleasant;
no malice has befallen like lightning.

You weep into your own lap.
Incidentally, it was Blake,
and a cold baked potato.

Poets and actors reign,
on the hillsides
and among the forests,
loom like the notion
of a merciless desert:
Arizona in dream.

On the television
everything is the sick romance of war,
an inevitable drama. All hail;
the lust for Glory!

So in what way
does my personal narrative
pertain to anything important?

Bah! The unwelcomed visitor,
the blessing
we are not accustomed to receiving.

In the small room in the back of the house,
I have not been frequent,
and everything here is old, and filthy,
and offensively out of fashion.

Gravity and/or Grace (After Simone Weil)

Today you are ailed, a person living
among the defects of the physical body.

I brew tea, sit alone with the comfort of words
while you sleep before a television
tuned to a channel
which broadcasts real life heart transplants
and the immediate suffering
that comes from injury
and the failure of certain bodily organs.

Show me where I can locate your void.
It occurs to me that when you consider
yourself as an entity with the same composition
as everyone else,
you are witness to your own comedy.

Am I oblivious of myself? Are you?
For whose sake
does night continue to fall and fall?

Suffering learned in infancy returns,
recalls itself as the essence of existing.

My newborn daughter cannot tell me
what is wrong in words.

She cries out, helpless under God,
thrashes her arms
in an attempt at some rough translation.

I am lung, brain, flesh, and the capacity
of sight and sound.

Beyond these things,
I am merely a mess of hopeless insights.

Snow in Boston, or Walking, Presently

Immense compunction floods
like a terrible clanging in the ear.
I have consumed items that shine.

A particular politic lingers,
real as a representation, faces which
transform into numbers, words,
stories that spread
and become spectacular
and worthy of the lively discourse
which ensues, dies, gets filed away
like a century.

It is a revolution and a literature.

It is my intermittent nap
on a Saturday afternoon, the luxury
of learning to speak French,
my newborn daughter
surfeited and bloated
from yet another feeding.

Lofty language bleeds from our mouths
like necessary editorials, each one
about storms that threaten
to gut the earth, to arouse the seas.

They are thrilling! They are incendiary foreplay,
a dark room which recollects
the beginning of some world, God
prior to his first decree. They thrill us,
thrill the infant and her glimmering eye,
thrill even the most indiscriminate insect.

I watch the insect creep along
the arm of the sofa. My whole history
is a city swarming with whores
and divergent and starry light. Look,

how the light bounces off a woman's blouse.
I know her, but she is not
a thing of language. She is an embodiment,
a parking lot
full of shiny new cars.

In some parts of Boston,
there are desolate nights,
and days with brash and brazen sun,
delirious with youth and idiocy,
the snow disordered and whirling.

The sun annihilates. It pinkens the cheeks,
makes you nothing. You traverse like fog,
glad in the person
you have proposed yourself to be.

It maps time and location
as absurd, so serious and absurd
that it hurts the brain, makes you deflect it,
forget it, recall it, like love or war,
or make perfect sense
of the pretty mobile that spins
around the head
of your newborn daughter.

She looks up, confused, grinning,
reaching for you with her tiny arms.

You are somebody, and you have
no idea who you are, except
that you go on, carry the purposes of each day
like a script. You are walking on a street

on your way to work. Strangers embrace you
as important and prospering. You are lost,
and delirious with the joy of it,
and things are only as familiar
as you have rendered them.

Winter, in a Photograph

My mind dwells in all Chekovian winters,
the dark before dawn
a holy calling to any altar of God.

Endurance illumines death.
I dwell in the pitted core
of a Chekovian winter, horses passing
like silhouettes, like iron carvings of horses
that you might set
to be admired on the mantle.

No candle burns
to mark the resolve of this anger,
no tempered flame
sustains the early evening.

Dread is a person inside a box,
and there are people in boxes
all over the world.

On the other hand, hope
is a hopeless notion.

It is something you must conjure
like genius that gently taps a drum,
my daughter's small hand
reaching for mine
while I sit in a box,
hysterically weeping.

Later, I take out the trash,
renounce the resonance of words,
show you a happy photograph
of two lovers in winter,
embracing.

Wind in Houses

A tea kettle is the wind through the cracks
in the walls of an abandoned house, mid-winter.
You are brewing tea as infants sleep,
as imaginations tick like clocks in kitchens.
Then, an interruption occurs.
There are sassy girls on the TV
singing about misters and jigs.
It is disquieting. I was thinking
about the unsteady streaming
of headlights at dusk, time slipping by
without suspicion or instance.
Then I considered justice, with or without
the shrewd activist. I mean academy.
The shrewd academy. The shrewd man
sitting in the kitchen sipping tea.
The shrewd revolution of kitchen literature.
The justice that prevails or does not.
The monotonous sound of a clock, or an infant
nodding off in a electronic swing
that sways and sways in either direction.
Some dichotomy of meaning.
The metaphysical mysticism of meaning.
The murder mystery of meaning.
My upstairs neighbor is pacing and pacing
above the ceiling. I am afraid
that she wants to die, that I have not offered her
mouthfuls and bounties of food. I am speaking
directly into the mouths of beasts.
The beasts are eating my superfluous language,
and the meaning is swallowed
by the age of near-darkness, the only light
a deception of the spirit.
The light is brief and catastrophic.
The light reminds us not to sleep.
An infant moves her small hands

like alphabets, in an effort to convey all of this.
Today, I read a book with a little boy
all about houses in forests,
and houses on mountains, and houses on water,
and houses in deserts. A house was depicted
on a beach, and the sand appeared as if like snow.
And the wind through the cracks
in the walls of the house, like lonely tea-kettles,
continues to sing and sing, and indefinitely sing.

Nocturne

Finally, morning inherits its alighted Alleluias.
There is an exquisite literature dropping
from your hands like rain. It makes me think
of mallards cast away from a lake
by winter ice, of singing nymphs
and intimate cups of coffee. It makes me think
of something that celebrates a dark night,
duly spotted with random light. It makes me think
of something crude and holy: the way
you take hold of the flesh on my ass, the way
your rage is the blur of oncoming traffic,
infused with a terrible passion, a blessed communion
that gives life to the dead.

And I cannot condemn it.
And I cannot drink it like a soul. Finally,
morning inherits its alighted Alleluias,
and our daughter is drowsy,
caught underneath the weight
of the subtle nocturnes that are cast
upon her heavy and inevitable eyes.

Plath in a Room: White Curtains and Televisions

I would enjoy anything antiquated that you might be offering:
cigarette smoke and typewriters, dresses with collars
that gather close around the neck. I enjoy your penmanship,
the elegant lines of your antiquated pen. Your children
are portraits with fire in their eyes, caught in time
by the helpless oblivion of youth. Now I can't stop wondering:
what was the ordering of your life? I saw a room
in a house today with white curtains, which seemed
very sane and regulated. Somehow, I was devastated,
filled with rage over the sofa and the white curtains.
I wanted to go there, lie down, and pretend to die.
The air in the room would not have been too cold.
The air would have been perfect, and sunlight
would have been a blinded glance. I would have been
lonely while my husband slept. The TV would have
been depicting people in previous decades.
The show would have been about baseball.
A bottle of milk would have fallen slack
from my daughter's mouth. I would have thought
about drinking tea, but I wouldn't have drunk it.
I would had to have kept things in better perspective.
I would had to have apologized to God.
My daughter would already have been speaking French.
I would have thought about nudity and booze.

I am completely responsible for my own identity.
When I think of being young,
everything is green and grassy, and there are nomads
traveling from house to house
in the name of the Lord.
Once, I had an accident with a car,
and I disturbed someone's life. I was forgiven.
Another time, I had an accident with a car,
and I was forgiven. Mercy survives us.
As recourse, I would sit in a dark room,
alone, and listen to the dim and distant sound
of a television that never sleeps.

Sometimes the Lord

Sometimes, the Lord is a blue night
with starry parameters.

On the TV a cartoon panda plays the flute.
My daughter coos in the late afternoon light
that breathes in the curtains.

Sometimes,
these things are also the Lord.

Alas, she yawns.
The world is a hysterical place.

Have faith in something
if only for lack of its evidence,
or just for the sake of vindicating
your own sorry heart.

This thing of faith
has no business in this world.
The wind was cold today
and it made my daughter scream.

And you are also screaming.

You are screaming politely.
You are screaming very quietly
and that is why
you are screaming your head off.

Sometimes the Lord
is a poor boy in field, filled with moonlight.
He is happy in spite of circumstance,
a beacon
that ogles the sky
in wonder, for no reason
that I can think of.

Portals

A woman is the recurrence of things.
Her body toils as its own mechanism.
In the late afternoon, an infant babbles
and coos among the dissipating sunlight.
There are skills required for this vocation:
a spinning wheel, a thread and needle,
the proper ratios of water.

After my afternoon nap,
I am lying in bed, unwillingly awake.
The world has its own investments.
If I lie here long enough,
will I recall my own existence?
I try to discuss things
with the vast and ambiguous "other."
An infant is an undercurrent,
a disorganized music, the world
in measured or unmeasured increments.

You contact the universe through portals.
The portals have inherited certain laws,
your language rough and effective.

I am scrubbing and scrubbing the kitchen floor
and it is a useless application.
The infant is my daughter.
She is coming to understand
the external aspects of everything.
Certain aspects are evident.
Certain aspects of you were thrilling,
and now they are necessary.

Maybe we could go to a coffee shop,
somewhere on the outskirts of Chicago perhaps?
Sit together, legs pressed, intimate as dusk.

It would be interesting to see
how the literature
might have transpired otherwise.

And yet life, with a name and beating heart,
is nodding off now, drowsy and contented
in my uncertain arms. Her foot moves,
as merely as an intention,
a car passes on the wet street outside,
like a wave on the sea.

No minute ticks for naught.

Soon, you will return,
and there will be the noise of you,
your voice, your thoughts like deconstructions,
warfronts of the imagination.

There will be the kiss on my mouth,
the kiss on the infant's high forehead.

The literature will pass like an evening
once the last glass is drunk,
as the portal widens and widens,
and the good world falls in.

A Child's Mouth

You might attribute it to winter, the cavernous
architecture of all longing. Though today,
there is no snow. Though today, no rare bird
comes to rest its wings in the yard.

We are moving, moving, filling the increments
that time has proffered. We are futurity,
in theory.

A child wonders what existed before the night.
A child tries to identify the sound of a cicada.
A child grows love like a deformed limb.

I must be death, because I am a mother's bosom.
And I am rocking my child, to and fro, against my body.
She sleeps to a solemn verse. She sleeps to the chaos of noise.
A blessing drifts in, and it is dismissed
in lieu of darkness.

I hate you. I love you; I hate you.
The world is a murder victim.
There are overtures and arousals,
 a soft radio, an intimate embrace
in a dirty kitchen.

I hate you. I love you. There are overtures.
There are four eggs left in the carton
for tomorrow morning. There is dusk;
a vanishing of light.

The distance is an ancient flute.
Let us go there, love, and be reacquainted.
Let us be nothing but tongues, all language
left for death, spring forthcoming
like a strange mania.

On my way to the liquor store this afternoon,
I thought deeply about deep things.
I was terse with the cashier.
It was bad for business.

I look at my child now, helpless as something that begins,
and does not know the implication of its ending.
She is beautiful: a preface to all language.

Her hand is resting gently on my breast,
as her exhausted mouth falls open,
and then open, like something that extends:
a duration, an instant, errant,
nearly eternal.

Voices

The King of all literature arrives at my front door
and he is wearing a green suit. He claims
the nuance of everything, the whispers
that are heard in all dark rooms:
your ubiquitous muse, the flute-song
that hails the ghosts of uncertain memory.
I want to be sure that what I am saying
inherits its own accuracies.
There are voices of the dead
carried by wind, and they are God.
Today a gust of it nearly blew us
into annihilation. I don't know quite what it is
that I continue to lament: the arrival
or the departure? Love drifts in,
lays its sword on the dirty table.
In the middle of the night, the power fails,
and the clock blinks like an irritation of light.
You enter me like an apology, a raging deer
in the winter. No shotgun sounds
to mark its own territory. In the quiet
of the evening, I think I hear
the attenuated voice of Plath:
carry on, carry on, like a chariot,
lest your fire should burn itself to death.

Despair upon Waking

Late at night, I wait for you in a room
like spring, its urgent rivers roiling
into distances. It is the dark
which is my refuge,
my mind without exact location,
a thing of verbosity.

It begins to reason with itself.
It discerns God, a trace of something dead,
that wild and inconspicuous angel.

Between me and my mind,
a solution has arisen.
I wait for you in a room,
like spring.

Earlier, we watched a show on the TV
about the corruption of the church,
the crimes and sins of ordinary priests.

I wasn't thinking about this.

Instead, I thought about
a photograph of my mother,
lying in the grass,
holding me above her head
as an infant. She was smiling
and her hair shined.

Later, you enter me like a room,
the dark my refuge, myself the refuge
and the dark, the shape of you
difficult to discern. I love you
like a reoccurrence, a repetition,
so many indiscriminate howls
of grief and desire.

Later, I dream that I am dead.

My mother
is a thing of consolation.

There is the moment of crucifixion,
and my newborn daughter floats
among some disorder
of scattered stars.

Misplacement

It seems that you have misplaced something.
A text underlies the business of this world,
enduring you, waking you out of sleep
in the middle of the night. It seems
that the text is all too familiar, too much
like dinner on the table at 6 pm, too much
like a kiss on mouth upon departure
or arrival. It seems I am shriveling
like age. There are misplaced objects:
your keys, the replaced wallet,
the critical stack of papers, a number
that looms like a distance
and furnishes your futurity. Snow fell today
and you mentioned Fellini.

Glamorous Parties

There was something about the hunk of bread
that made me want to embody
something morose and desperate
under a streetlamp, the mist
from after a rainstorm
efflorescing in the wan light.

Something blue, with gothic hair
surrounding my tidy face, decadent smoke
expelled from between my lips.

Something that starves and sings alto
in a dark bedroom.
How I enjoy these glamorous grandeurs
by proxy, by a lonely house
just a few yards
from a dirty river.

There is an ecstasy of God
so bright
that this world
is merely relevant in passing,
as an afterthought.

My body
recalls all previous pain
in the womb, the soul
raging in want of light.

Today I saw my newborn daughter's
first real tear
swell in her left eye, real as death
or the sea in winter.

Meanwhile, Clara Schumann played and played
the way that solitude plays the mind
when you are gone.

Adagio in G

It would be futile to argue about such matters.
You play for me someone's Adagio in G
and all of the horrible, horrible aspects of the world
come to harbor in my soul, desperate, like Pandora,
to be released, to make desperation sing.

I want to give you things, like an infant's small foot
keeping time with the music
as you hold her against you for dear life,
for injustices that claim us like something that starves,
like something that wails and wails
to become a conception.

This world has the stench of countless transits,
of opinions that rise to each occasion
and then become oblivious, some idle chatter
that lingers, for example, in an empty barroom,
the remaining patrons
slurring like words in the near-darkness.

I want you like a terrible catastrophe, the unrelenting rain,
the Adagio in G, all of these accidents
which generate life.

Take these things like stones.
Like accidents, like something that you can transfigure
into twisted birds that represent
all the joy and sickness of the spirit.

Keep them like compiled notes: like intentions
for something subsequent.

Roads

That it was no country at all, but an expanse
of divine roads, stretching
between here and the horizon: the pavement
a metaphor for the passage of time, whirling
in and out of cities
where the people are never the same.

God save them all for their obvious desires.
God save them and their taxes, their gardens
sleeping in the yards
underneath the February snow.

And mine, as well: no I am not good enough
to lack deflections, not to blaspheme, to be immune
to my own stench of womanhood.
The air brightens after dawn,
in the morning outside the church
where we go
to greet our Lord,
where we discuss things
with strangers
like the danger of slipping
on winter ice.

My knees can never be holy enough.
I am a void in want of justice, a person drifting
like an incidence. I swallow and swallow wine
in hope of some vast and magical ascension.

My little daughter sleeps like the silence
and the day deadens into darkness.

Tomorrow, we will resume
our travels, redemptive as roads.

As if the time you first touched me,
pulled over in a back lot, the blues humming
like a low radio, everything fast and blurry
as the world.

Impetus

Eventually your will is going to get the better of you,
like a gusty wave in the sea.

You will move
toward something, or away.

There will be facilities of desire
for objects, a passion for things
that are other than you,
and that you see reflected
as necessities of longing.

Yes, to "long:" in other words
an intolerable July, distances like love
seen at a drunken hour,
the warm rain at night
clean and holy
as a mother.

Birth is the cry
of a prior language.

After that, we just learn the necessary scripts,
arise like the noise of beasts
out of darkness.

Valentine's Poem

I am drawn, like a light to the surface of water, close to
our Lord. His eyes are downcast and steady as rain, like a
person standing in the rain as an act of defiance—like rain
that spills in through an open window and soaks an entire
shelf full of books. Like rain that keeps you awake at night.
Last night I dreamt that the police found me in the midst
of disobedience. The road was dark and I was driving too
fast. It must have been pouring. This morning the ritual of
coffee was a lapse of endurance. A nail through the hand?
It is Valentine's Day and I have songs for you, to sweeten the
ear, to distract you from the heavy world. Good morning!
Yesterday, I saw a young girl carrying a cello as she strolled
to school. Today, I saw the same girl, but this time, she was
carrying a clarinet. There is a multitude of days left for you,
for me. Today I am filing taxes. Tomorrow, I will see the
physician. The minute is busy, the mind divided between
this thing and that. "You can gain the whole world, but lose
your place in heaven." Heaven is spot on the brain filled
with blinding sun, with eggs sunny-side up and peaceful
patios. Heaven is the crickets on a warm night, the noise
buzzing through the wooden blinds. Last night I dreamt
that I had lost track of where my little daughter was. I asked
someone, and the person drove us backwards in her car
into a random storefront. When I woke up, my daughter
was sleeping soundly beside me, her breath a series of stac-
cato notes, expelled. Thank you, O—wherever you are.

Valentine's Day Poem #3

If you itemized all the numbers you were meant to remember, the math would be astronomical. It is life without a face, your name in automation. Nobody knows that you are cooking spaghetti tonight, that you prefer gardenias to roses, that your menses has been delayed this month. Nobody knows that you wanted to erect an entire circus in your front yard when you were young, that you wrote your deepest dreams on stones and submerged them in the sewer every Sunday. You loved the cluster of the lilac bush, the typical book, the languor of a summer day. What necessitated time aside from the dream of adulthood, out there like a distance? Now, the numbers are utilized to identify the texture of your bones. People are friendly like obligations and appropriated sunlight. Darling, you are the threshold of desperation, a prayer for a tall glass. Why do you weep in the heart of darkness, in the unbearable light? You are trying to follow a precarious line, like a duty. I love you. Go to the river where the water is immense. There are blessings there, like terrible whispers.

Tall Hotels

It is because you are absolutely right,
correct in your seeming chaos
like a perfect and determinate arrow.
How it leads me as if a diversion, a digression,
straight into the expansive loins of all desire.
Semiotics attributes me to some
sublimated sense of being good:
my skirt fashionably pious
and draped duly below the knee.
Today, all self-righteous proclamations
proved me an imposter, and I resolved
to my own idiocy: previously covert, unwitting,
previously unwilling to notice itself.
So I purposely make a mess of the house,
scatter my clothing all over the floor
and regard all food as disgusting and necessary.
I hold my newborn daughter above my head
and stupidly sing. How do we compensate
for our sufferings? By diversion.
By deflection, by digression.
Sirens outside rage like the night.
The lights in the house are on and blaring,
and fancy hotels glitter in the sky
like finalities. There is priceless art
on the walls there. There are girls
threatening to leap from balconies.
Everyone claims their own
profitable decadence, photograph
their lovers in red light, appear beautiful
in their sacred transience. The poetry
simply slurs from drunken tongues,
and we feel useful. And my mind
is swift like train, passion
not dissipated, my soul
both ugly and alive.

Poet Man

What difference is there in anything
if not the perishable body? Things light up
in the dark, spectacular as science.
Some of them are the heads of holy men.
Some of them were bought on discount.
I hear the inexhaustible despair
of someone in longing for God.
It is a cry that pales the face, draws lines
in the fevered forehead. It is a soft piano
only heard in certain proximities.
A man of music is a purgatory
in search of heaven.

Snow Falling

It is said
that in some stories,
snow falls
on a dark world.
When I look
outside the window
I see the light and currency
of a city. The geography
is elusive. I consider
the sky and the earth
and feel
somehow irrelevant.
The television swells
with suppositions of life,
maintains
its tireless narrative.
Here: meaning is inherited
by way of ignorance,
by way of its own
usual gimmicks.
A man leaps from a building
and Hollywood has the rights:
tragedy finally observed
in a warm room
with tea and expensive sofas
while the snow falls
outside
on a dark world.

Events

At first, there was terrible rain, thunder that deafened the eardrums. Various means of shelter were coveted. Dogs recalled their own ancestry. They howled. They growled and snarled at the guests. People considered guns as resolutions for rage. People considered metaphors as resolutions for rage. There were words, vicious as tongues. There were blackened eyes, and faces awash with tears. Children were caught like casualties amid the war of words, amid the war of fists and sexes. There were men of God and there were men of magazines. Someone's heart grew like a revolution, like a wound. The wound was revered. It was poetic, humorous, entertaining at occasions which involved wine and gourmet cheese. The music was hip. Some people thought so with such passionate intensity that they broke guitars. They broke violins. They broke the expressions on some people's faces. The war proliferated like neighborhoods, like families, like vacations in exotic places. A fire burnt down the city. And then everyone involved got into their warm cars and drove around, with no particular destination in mind, and thought a lot about what happened for awhile.

An Ear, the Forest, Or?

I am meant to be a shadow
in the shape of a tree. The issue is.
I dreamt this, and some ambitious commentary
about the 1920s. I'm sure
that some very important people witnessed this,
stuffed their mouths
with some variety of shellfish. The room
was dimly lit, the guests wont
to a drunk ecstasy. Everything seemed
critical as a trailing of eloquent words.
I woke to the sound of a desperate child,
your desire for the eternal breaking point
temporarily housed in the silence of sleep.
They said this was necessary.
God is long road, the pavement paled
with early sunlight. It is cold
and the inside of my mouth feels insipid.
I would like a glass of water.
The issue is. A saint only arises
out of inevitable things. You return home
having hauled a whole mountain
on your back. I speak to the desperate child
in Hebrew inflections, the music
rising like the timbres
of your unquiet soul. The issue is.
A sense of the unquiet soul reverberates
off of these lonely walls. I noticed this morning
that the wallpaper was tearing.
It was beautiful, squalid, something
to note like an occasion. It is a cause
for discussion. God is a long road,
a longing for intimate discussions.
The desperate child sleeps in the midst
of dissent, her body
expanding like breath. I would like

a glass of water. But play that music
one more time. It is like blood in crisis.
It is orgasmic, pivitol, a breaking point
that sings like something violate
in an abiding ear.
And the ear is the forest, in the dark,
where everything is holy and complicated.
Sometimes, in the forest
there is rain, the mind escaped to nothing,
and I cannot relent
in these offerings of grace.

Rising

Because at this point,
there were a thousand broken camels
in a distant desert. There was a need
for some exoneration.
The broken camels moaned.
The straw was unforgiving.
The moaning sounded like singing
in the heavy heat of the sun.
Because when there is no problem,
there is a problem
because there is no problem, and that
is the heart of the problem.
It is unnerving.
There is a problem
with the unsettled heart
and it longs to live
like sleeping dolphins in the sea.
I go to God unarmed
and ask to be redeemed
by anything
cool and dark.
Are you there?
My love, each breath
is small disturbance
and it is as eloquent as life.
There is evidence of life.
Each time I laugh
I am secretly terrified.
When you sang,
something was raised.

Asleep

The world she knows when she is but asleep:
quiet conversation and gunshot, the noise

of sex and televisions, the rush of rain.
And the end of everything is the sea,

and all iniquity is banished, like a mortal,
like manifestations of earthly rage.

In a bedroom, there are visions of corruption,
dreams of interactions in parking lots,

heads full of contemplation and voices.
For now my love, please remain asleep.

For now, the music continues
like the world, even after the blood

of death. The world she knows
when she is but asleep: dim light

and a terrible murmur
of discontent.

Perspective (for Another Woman)

Once, you were all too good: a thin sounding bell
in some incidental song. It was pretty.
It had hope, promise. It was a promise
that was as green as a summer field.
Then, you began to understand yourself
as desire, and you held your breath
until you were blue, set yourself off running,
off and off, like a horizon.
Did they ever tell you
that the horizon was the ghost of the horizon?
A trace of something certain
which begs to deceive you, something
illusory, a wicked bargain like a perfect coin?
Myths, myths, a mouth that is empty of screaming.
The coin shines, is persuaded like an eye.
The mouth is the mouth of a dragon.
It is dirty like a word.
It threatens like a new perspective,
but you refuse to hear it.

After the Wedding

I'm sure that I mentioned the fishing pole and the whiskey,
the dawn spent walking through the fog
that drifts from the lake. The quiet room, the window,
the budding trees, a flourish of something yellow or blue.
Last night, I thought I might also have mentioned
that I was as brief as a candle. She mentioned
the drapes up in the flames, the budding of love or trees,
everything new like a distance, unreal, proposed
like a life. The house was as quiet as a sleeping infant.
A digression, a world unto its own world.
You were a cluster of henna blossoms. Once or twice,
there was the sound of breaking glass.

Drift

1
February was a song once, and it made you inspired.
You envisioned a particular brand of survival.

Back then, the house was small, my womb vacant,
the passing of days
gradual and drunk, like something young:
a meal in the midst of a garden
in the setting sun.

I'm sure that Rod Stewart
had something to do with it, I mean
with respect to the coordinates
of burgeoning love.

Like I said, it was young.

There was new terror, an abundance of birds,
a mind both busy and unacquainted.

2
Presently the meal is served, exuberant
and well-designed. Something falls apart,
but it is beautiful.

I just can't stop letting go
of my former self, its distant shadow of life.

There is a reflection of a flame
in the window.

My love I have come to know
like the absent routine
of sweeping a floor, like discourse
and blood.

3
Friends drift in like coincidences,
the loveliest leaves of a forthcoming spring.

L, S, my gratitude for the city-walks of the mind,
the terror and delight of an impossible prairie,
all the last suppers of the waning winter.

L, S, Oh Ring of Fire, the coffee has spilled.

4
My love, something has drifted
and departed.

It came with words, and left with words.

Here is the remaining Word,
you lying here next to me,
consumed in breath, the Word,
the Word
in the Deadest Sea.

Bequeathing (for Joe and Clare)

Traffic of winter trees in the dark. All things collapsed
and then begun. How can I want you
like these distances
even while you lie this close? The moon
is perfect, like an egg, like the ever-present eggs
of pesach & spring, eggs galore, eggs presiding,
eggs presuming all the previous labors
of my body. It hurts. Did I mention that it hurts?
And here we are rejoicing, rejoicing,
drinking gin on a Tuesday evening. The Lord said to me:
thou shalt not dare bring any further suffering
into this house. This house is the house
of exploding love. And the love explodes like a face.
In the morning, the Lord, and a cup of coffee.
The rain is not iniquity. Not iniquity. The rain
is refuge from all things ugly and terrifying.
It is the good hour of midnight, your chest
a subtle gesture as you sleep, rising and falling
in the dark. But for this small light. This small light,
this child, bequeathed like a season, a star.

Dear Clare

Dear Clare, I wonder if one day you will know
that the winter trees shivered with rain on the day you were born.
That the letter "P" is the first letter in the word "place."
On the television, they're showing mutt-dogs
and emphasizing the number 3, over and over
in game-show intonations.

You're eating lunch or sleeping in the afternoon,
and the cookie monster is eating the letter "H."
P+H equals philosophy, equals the miracle
of sperm+egg, swimming in the blind universe of a woman,
equals the phenomenon of the habitual seasons,
the mystery of gray hair and eventual aging.

Spring breaks everything open like a heart, or fractured shale.

Dear Clare, I wonder if one day you will know
that poetry can often be as basic as a bank receipt,
the reason your mother turns her back to your restless limbs
before bed, and buries her head in the darkest "place"
she can find.

Ink-blue air fills my head like a distress call
for all things filled with nothing.

Existence is God's foolery, a conundrum
that wearies the currencies of living breath, the blood-beat
of task and routine.

Arbitrary numbers consume the ridiculous railways of my mind,
words full of disorder, words full of their own words,
voices that speak as if through a hollow glass. God?

He informed me of thievery, of servants
or zombie cash-registers trafficking here and there,
dutiful as Sisyphus.

I feel Sisyphus in the very undoing of me,
the imagination of my bones, ligaments,
the thresholds that live and die
under the surfaces of my skin.

Dear Clare, I wonder if one day you'll remember
that silly monster on the television, singing to his trebled piano.
Do you remember the illusion of wild animals and birds?
Children explaining the phenomenon of lunchtime?

You are eating your lunch, have fallen asleep
with your face in your sweet potatoes.
Will you remember your baby brother's mysterious difference—
the curious tenors of his wailing?

Will you remember trash, the budding of trees,
your mother tipping the wine like some ecstatic Judy Garland?
Will you remember the faint beckoning of the Holy Ghost?
The wind through the blinds while you sleep?
The early morning darkness? The vague arithmetic of infancy?
The nice looking man, repeating words
that begin with the letter "N?"

N is for Naples, nonsense, Nicene Creed.
"I believe in God, the father almighty,
Creator of heaven and earth, of all things visible and invisible."

Visible is the blue and ignorant sky. The all-knowing eye,
the vacant and haunting elsewhere.

Invisible is why I even began to write this poem,
the love that kills me
and never stops bringing me home.

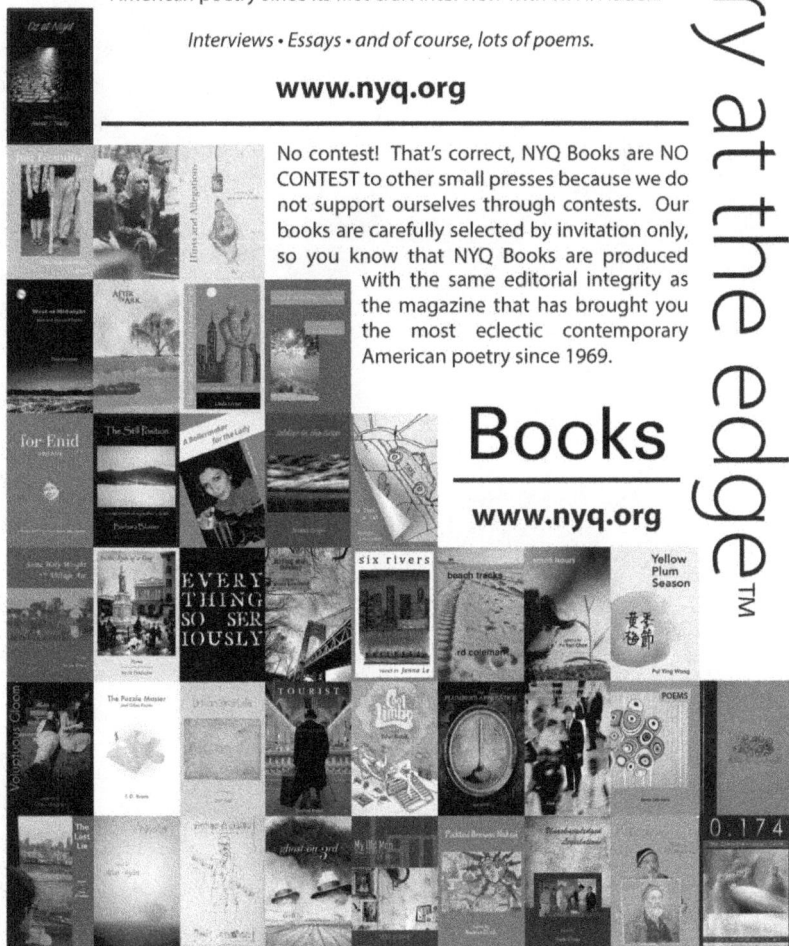

www.ingramcontent.com/pod-product-compliance
Lightning Source LLC
LaVergne TN
LVHW091230080426
835509LV00009B/1233